The Air Transport Auxiliary (ATA)

The Air Transport Auxiliary – unofficially known as Ancient and Tattered Airmen, Always Terrified Airwomen or Anything to Anywhere – was a civilian organisation founded at the outbreak of World War II to ferry planes between factories, maintenance units and frontline squadrons and was vital to the role of the RAF. There were 1,246 ATA aircrew, including 164 women and four female engineers, from over 25 countries. Pilots had no instruments or radios and were at the mercy of the British weather and enemy aircraft.

Pauline Gower was the driving force behind the newly formed women's section and was based at the ATA's headquarters at White Waltham. The First Eight were recruited on New Year's Day 1940, initially to fly training aircraft such as Tiger Moths, but in July 1941 women were cleared to fly operational aircraft – all fighter types including Spitfires and Hurricanes and twin engines such as Mosquitos and Wellingtons.

There were three all-women ferry pools (Hamble, Cosford and Hatfield) and women achieved equal pay in 1943. Four of the First Eight received MBEs and two women were awarded Certificates of Commendation.

A valuable collection of log books, diaries and photographs is held at the Maidenhead Heritage Centre near White Waltham, which is regarded as the spiritual home of the ATA.

Acknowledgements

My thanks and appreciation to everyone who has helped me along the runway of research and writing: Sue Rose for her valuable aviation advice; Anne Grant for the Solent Aviatrix website and links; Pauline Vahey for including poetry as part of the British Women Pilots' Association Diamond Jubilee weekend; Candida Adkins, daughter of Jackie Moggridge, for sharing her family memories and giving me copies of her mother's poems; Elizabeth Harrison MBE for memories of her friend and pilot Monique Agazarian; Jacky Hyams (*The Female Few*) for her encouragement; Midge Gillies (*Amy Johnson, Queen of the Air*) for her support; staff and volunteers at Brooklands Museum and to Richard Poad, Chairman of Maidenhead Heritage Centre, for his time, anecdotes and the opportunity to fly their Spitfire Simulator – which is highly recommended!

I am grateful for the support of the National Lottery through Arts Council England for what has proved to be a hugely rewarding and ongoing project.

Thanks and gratitude also to Dawn Bauling and Ronnie Goodyer at Indigo Dreams for wanting to share these remarkable women's stories as much as I did.

A Touch of Silk, 3pm Appointment at Austin Reed and Moving Up the Blackboard were published in *The Lake*. On Such a Day and Washing Our Hair appeared in *London Grip*.

Other publications by Alison Hill

Slate Rising, IDP, 2014
Lyrical Beats (ed), Rhythm & Muse, 2012
Peppercorn Rent, Flarestack, 2008

Sisters in Spitfires

Alison Hill

First Edition: Sisters in Spitfires
First published in Great Britain in 2015 by:
Indigo Dreams Publishing
24, Forest Houses
Cookworthy Moor
Halwill
Beaworthy
Devon
EX21 5UU

www.indigodreams.co.uk

ISBN 978-1-910834-00-8

British Library Cataloguing in Publication Data. A CIP record for this book can be obtained from the British Library.

Designed and typeset in Palatino Linotype by Indigo Dreams.
Cover design by Ronnie Goodyer. Cover photo: Diana Barnato Walker climbs into the cockpit of a Spitfire, 1945.
© Bill Cross/Rex Shutterstock, Author photo: David Hobbs.

Printed and bound in Great Britain by 4edge Ltd.

Papers used by Indigo Dreams are recyclable products made from wood grown in sustainable forests following the guidance of the Forest Stewardship Council.

Dedicated to all those who flew in the
Air Transport Auxiliary (ATA)

"To sit in the cockpit of a Spitfire, barely wider than one's shoulders, with the power of the Merlin at one's fingertips, was a poetry of its own."
Lettice Curtis

"A few seconds later I found myself soaring through the air in a machine that made poetry of flight…"
Jackie Moggridge (nee Sorour)

CONTENTS

Private Lives

Making the Headlines

Ferry Pilot's Notes

Sisters in Spitfires

Leaving Legacies

Sisters in Spitfires

PRIVATE LIVES

They flew through my dreams, nudging me awake with their stories.

A Trail of Oranges

For Pauline Gower and her school friend

She'd climbed every tree in the grounds
and leapt from every dormitory window;
the scent of oranges, hidden beneath

bloomers, recalling a stolen afternoon
up and over the high school walls
towards a delicious taste of freedom.

Shaking off regulations, bouncing curls
heralding friendship and laughter; a pair
on the cusp of just-around-the-corner.

Strolling through the market, selecting
their fare, the afternoon languished ahead.
Yet the chime of the church clock conjured

nuns' impatience, the sharp tang of incense.
Leaping back over the wall, straight to chapel
Pauline was mortified to feel her elastic give,

half-turning to spot a steady trail of oranges
rolling down the aisle. One came to rest beside
Sister Agatha's shoe. She declined to notice.

A Touch of Silk

I packed my parachute
I packed my evening gown –
what more did I need?

My *Gone with the Wind* dress
I called it, essential for a girl
dashing about in a plane.

We never knew when glamour
might beckon – a dinner, a dance,
so I packed it just in case –

patting down the soft red velvet
cushioned against the tough
parachute straps of *silk & security*.

Dorothy Furey was one of the first American woman hired by the ATA. Flying for her was an 'interesting interlude'; she went on to breed race horses and take up scuba diving at the age of seventy-seven.

Washing Our Hair

The sky was literally a washout –
the day had been declared one.

Some despatched to the nearest pub,
others to find a decent meal.

I needed some time alone and
grounded, some space to think.

Time to enjoy the simple ritual
of washing, rinsing, towelling –

scanning myself in the cracked
mirror above the sink, slick a curl

or two in their place, paint a smile,
feign a shrug before an early night.

Pears soap too, if I was lucky –
Preparing to be a Beautiful Lady

Not much time to prepare really,
but now and then it did us good

to remember our skin, our hair,
what lay beneath our golden wings.

Margot's Wings

Turned the singer's voice to honey,
crooning a love song from centre stage
to a navy uniform on the balcony.

She held the theatre in her palm,
Margot pinned to her seat, the ballad
arousing the storm before the calm.

Margot's wings were on fire, caught
in the spotlight, while the woman sang
of lingering love, a girl in every port.

Mock consternation when the lights
went up and she spied Margot's blushes,
felt the audience ripple with delight.

Women in uniform were still of note,
what she hadn't bargained for, clearly,
were women with wings on their coat!

Margot Gore MBE was one of only two female Commanding Officers in the ATA (Hamble 1941-45).

Model Pilot, Model Lawn

For Monique Agazarian

The Sacred Heart sisters found her a *delightful*
child but very pleasure-loving. Peter Pan inspired
dreams of flying, lent her silver-tipped wings.

Her passion for planes began in the back garden,
in an old Sopwith Pup her mother found at auction;
Monique and her brothers happily flew the world.

From volunteer nurse to ferry pilot, Monique stood
taller for the ATA, borrowing an inch or three
for her medical, flying Spitfires with ease.

She ferried cigarettes once or twice too, stashed
in an overnight bag or down by her parachute,
a welcome favour for those waiting to fly.

Long after the war she manicured her window box
with nail scissors; a friend's flight of fancy adding
a miniature blue Spitfire set into the grass.

She'd flown all types of front-liners in the war,
yet did not take a coach trip until May 1991.
Why be driven when you can fly?

Monique wanted the sound of a Merlin engine
at her funeral – *arriving, passing, fading* –
lingering essence of her energy, her vibrant life.

Taking Tea with Thomas Hardy

And the visiting lady is all abloom,
And says there was never so sweet a room

I was shy, but it was not as bad
as matchmaking – I liked to think
I had some literary credentials!

And Thomas didn't mind a fig
if I was near-blind or lame;
I was just a young girl perched
 on a tapestry wing-back.

But I could sense he was trying hard
to remember my name and how
I fitted into his landscape.

I tried to imagine his books, his desk,
his pen, hoping I may inspire a line or two,
the angle of my cheek or my face in repose.

Before I found planes I dived into books,
hid deep beneath their pages, as later
I skimmed the feathered clouds
 solo in my Cirrus Moth.

Mary de Bunsen's heart was 'rather an odd shape for a Mosquito pilot' and she suffered from childhood polio and poor sight. She hummed Bach fugues as she ferried Spitfires; flying was her passion.

When Lettice Borrowed a Bicycle

She insisted on the Royal Canadian at Taplow,
not Slough, the day she force-landed a Typhoon,
the day she smashed her face and gashed her leg –
not a pretty sight. People had quickly materialised,
the ambulance crew muttering *it's Saturday afternoon.*

They took her to White Waltham, Lettice still insisting
on the Canadian. She got her own way, but was left to
walk in alone. Luckily Lady Astor was visiting that day –
You young things! – and dashed off to find a doctor
to sew up the patient's head at her polite request.

She was put in a side ward, where she rested properly for
the first time in four years. A few of the more able-bodied
nipped down to The Feathers in the evening and Lettice
was keen to join them, but when told of her impending
departure she explored the grounds instead.

She borrowed a bicycle, flying by pheasants parading
on the river bank, on through the woods. Undressed
and back in bed again, she was ready for supper at six.
Only the bicycle, leaning a little haphazardly, knew the
force of nature that had graced its well-worn saddle.

Lettice Curtis ferried almost 1,500 aircraft for the ATA including more than 400 heavy bombers. A founding member of the British Women Pilots' Association, she had a long flying career and gained her helicopter licence at the age of seventy-seven.

Waiting at the Gates

Marion smoothed the gravel and straightened her skirt,
trying not to check her watch for the umpteenth time.

She'd waited six long months with no letters, no calls,
no visual contact. She'd flown her Cirrus Moth, kept busy,

but the months had passed slowly, wondering which
life he wanted, whether they would ever marry.

The monastery door swung open on the clang of twelve
and there he was, smiling as he strode towards her.

He'd chosen her over God and she exhaled in relief,
her legs gaining strength as she met him halfway.

Twelve years later, Marion Wilberforce became one of only eleven women in the ATA to fly four-engined bombers. She gave up flying, reluctantly, at the age of eighty when she sold her second Hornet Moth.

Out of the Silence Came Chopin

She flew Spitfires with ease but never mastered
the gentle art of pedalling on two wheels.
Ann Welch on pilot Barbara Wojtulanis

We'd been practising in poor weather –
our wings clipped, we turned to two wheels,
running along the peri-track, Barbara wobbling
at my side, never quite getting her balance right –
it was so different in the air!
We grinned through gritted teeth, but it was
not to be and her cycle gave way to the Spit,
graciously bowing out of the duel.

Grounded again, just before Christmas,
we passed Winchester cathedral wreathed
in snow, lit only by the stars. Chopin's
Revolutionary Study cascaded through the silence
from a distant piano and Barbara was rooted
by strains of Polish hope.
The music ended as suddenly as it arrived,
leaving us shrouded in the snow-bound night.

Diana's Nine Lives

Diana Barnato Walker delivered 260 Spitfires and many twin-engined bombers during the war. She was convinced she had a guardian angel in the form of a badly burnt pilot who flung himself on her plane before her first solo flight at Brooklands. He kept her mind focused …

The Powder Puff Moment

I tried a roll in the Spitfire, but somehow got stuck upside-down at 5,000 feet and out flew that silver compact from my top pocket, showering the cockpit, the controls, the pilot … The striking Flight Lieutenant striding to meet me stopped short in his tracks – I was *not* the girl he was expecting, just a powder-puff clown! He turned on his heels and drove off …

The Bomb in the Basement

By some strange coincidence, my father put his foot down that night, telling me I was treating the place like a hotel. He was quite right, but I'd never say so. We stayed in, the three of us, and later learnt that my club of so many happy memories had been hit by a rogue bomb – down a vent, into the basement. We shuddered as we thought what might have been.

Bullets over Berkshire

There were twelve of us packed like sardines in the Anson, heading back to White Waltham. I was next to Jim Mollison in the co-pilot's seat. We may have been a little overweight, but weren't planning an overnighter. We hadn't bargained on a Jerry gunner aiming at us though! We hid in the overcast for as long as we dared before all piling out to look for bullet holes …

The Greenhouses and the Tractor

Delivering my 13th Spitfire, I should have been ready for
something to happen ... I was off to Essex and a murky mist
forced me to detour. I headed for a red dot of an aerodrome,
so small I had to fly low over some greenhouses and caused a stir,
the crowd was delighted I'd seen the man on the tractor ...
I bluffed my way out, with halo, tractor and greenhouses intact.

Cushions to Clear a Windsock

My first Hampden was unforgettable – it was a plane for a
long-legged pilot, not for little old me. For once the flight crew
were unhelpful – no cushions ... If only they could have seen
me dicing with death! I wedged my jacket, parachute and log
books behind me, but the G force whipped the throttle lever out
of reach. I missed the incoming windsock with inches to spare.

Mustang Waltz in a Pixie-Hood

It was a lovely day and I dipped the Mustang wings in time
with my own waltz, my hair cascading from the red pixie-hood
that had been the only thing I'd found to replace my broken
helmet. I was suddenly boxed in by four Spitfires in formation,
laughing Free Frenchmen keeping me on course to Kenley.
Been out with the boys I'd say, when Ops queried my delay.

Going Over the Top

It seemed the only option, taking a Spit from Eastleigh
to Cosford, flying over sunny Worcester. If I was spared
of course, as the next thing I knew I was in thick cloud.
I broke the rules, went on up to 12,000 feet... saw a gap
and dived, nose down, fingers virtually crossed. Vera
Strodl knew what I'd done – she'd been over the top too ...

A Wing and a Prayer

Sun to cloud, it was another of those days… I was enjoying the Spitfire IX, with the Cotswolds safely beneath me, when we struck cloud… Max and Billy's recent lesson swam though my head, *if in doubt, bale out,* but I was wearing a *skirt* and couldn't sail down in a parachute, showing off my hitched-up navy serge! My landing was memorable, my knees collapsed.

A Night in Silken Sheets

Flying a Mosquito, I ran into a heavy snowstorm and landed gingerly at Chilbolton. I was offered a bed in an empty Nissen, complete with the Colonel's very own silk sheets! Just the drip on the roof to send me to sleep. I woke unable to move, with a corporal at my side. The roof had collapsed and he'd come to my aid – a guardian angel with a shovel and a hot cup of tea!

Diana flew her own light aircraft after the war, encouraging young women to join the Women's Junior Air Corps. In 1963, at the age of forty-five, she became the first British woman to break the sound barrier. She gave the Minister of Defence twelve reasons why she should fly an RAF Lightning, 'I don't see why she shouldn't,' he said. (Spreading My Wings, 2003)

MAKING THE HEADLINES

The pilots of the RAF's most exclusive squadron reported for duty yesterday. They are eight girls... dressed in neat navy suits, with golden-braid wings on breast pockets, forage caps and fur-lined boots, these girl pilots took their seats in the cockpits of four RAF trainer planes and showed the men a thing or two about flying.

Daily Mirror, January 11, 1940

Do Air Women Lack Charm?

Enquired the *Daily Express* in 1936 – Harold Gatty,
round-the-world pilot and pioneer thought so.
The women in question were quick to respond.

Amy Mollison (nee Johnson) took his remark
as a personal insult, challenging him to a flight
'under any conditions HE cares to name'.

Society girl Jill Wyndham politely requested
an introduction next time he was in England –
she'd show him just how charming *she* could be.

Dorothy Spicer, Amelia Earhart and Pauline Gower
were also part of his press enquiry. Not women
to be taken lightly, they had more pressing issues.

Wanted: women pilots with over 600 flying hours,
engineering experience, solo flights to Australia
under their belt, grace, brains *and* charm. *Indeed!*

The Cover Girl

Maureen Dunlop was caught
on the cover of *Picture Post*
stepping fresh from a plane.
A breeze ruffling her curls,
she graced every breakfast
table, set many hearts aflame.

It was a perfect press moment,
unscripted, and they knew it.
She was forever that girl from
the plane, one hand to her hair
cap and goggles in the other,
an image of carefree glamour.

She'd told the photographers
she was busy, had a Barracuda
to put away, but then smoothed
her hair, smiled as the sun flared
her youth, her golden bracelet,
and there she was – cover girl!

Some Slight Confusion

Their hands may be small and their voices soft …
yet the 25 ATA women pilots *might easily be men*
declared the *Evening News* in February 1941.

They were all in it together – same uniform,
same hours, same regulations, at first less pay.

Theirs is a job in which an ounce of grit outweighs
a ton of glamour.

Yet Rosemary Rees, one of the feted First Eight,
saw it as an *appalling burden of responsibility*

flying anything to anywhere alongside the men
with huge pressure from press and public –

they had to show what they were made of, every
flight, every day; nothing less would do.

Courage Counts, Not Glamour
Evening News, 20 February 1941

This time the paper was onto something.
It took courage to travel halfway across
the world, in their twenties, from Chile,
Poland, South Africa, America and more,
often without much English, much money
or the right sort of clothes. Courage to take
a test flight, courage to say yes to the ATA,
courage to fly any number of types of plane
with only the Ferry Pilot's Notes at hand.
Courage to climb into unknown cockpits,
sit on parachutes they hadn't practised using.
Glamour yes, for most women at heart –
but only when the time was right, or the day
long enough for dinner, a dance or two
and a heady cocktail of wartime spirit.
But courage, courage was all.

Tiger Moth Scramble

The press had an airfield day, arriving at
Hatfield to capture those 'ACE Woman Pilots'
taking our jobs, according to some men.

*(They're getting good money for this –
£8 a week, I'm told.* One RAF pilot grumbled
to the *Daily Express … and why not?)*

The First Eight were photographed in full
flying gear, panting and laughing as the press
didn't catch them properly the first time.

So they had to run to their Tiger Moths again,
in brand new flying suits and fur-lined boots
with 30lb parachutes on their shoulders.

Maybe it was their field day?

In Defence of Ferrywomen

Responding to 'A Rank Scandal', February 2, 1940

Readers of *The Aeroplane, The most influential aviation journal in the world,* did not always agree with the renowned editor Mr C G Grey – some, it seemed, welcomed the arrival of the Atagirls.

One declared the women to be *types we want in this War* who should have the chance do to *useful War work.*

> *If by the end of the War they have ousted us from our jobs, it will be… up to us to go one better. Time enough to start our male protection society.*

Another reader suggested that lack of work for pilots was *one of the trials of War,* regardless of sex.

He (one can infer) concluded that it was *entirely sex prejudice on the part of Mr Grey* and challenged him to suggest how better the *undoubted flying experience of these ladies could be employed, or should they be idle and unused for the duration?*

Fortunately, they were not…

When Mrs Roosevelt Came to Lunch

Umbrellas were the order of the day at White Waltham,
as the heavens opened and stayed that way.

October '42 and fur-clad Mrs Roosevelt took a hustle tour
of the airfield, with Mrs Churchill and Mrs Hobby.

Lettice sheltered under the giant Halifax, while Pauline,
on walkabout duty, was drenched twice.

A full American lunch and questions for the First Lady
were disrupted by Moaning Minnie, a retreat to the shelter.

After the Daily Routine Order of full dress (no slacks),
and a hangar of tempting food, this was a bit much.

There was some speculation about a tip-off – maybe
the wet weather had worked to their advantage.

It was later discovered they'd bombed another airfield,
but the press latched onto one story the next day –

Girl Flies Halifax – it was only a matter of time.

FERRY PILOT'S NOTES

To fly all the different aircraft in the ATA we had Ferry Pilot's Notes, small cards held in a stiff cover by a shoelace ... No long-winded instructions on how to fly, just important facts such as approach speed, how to manage the fuel and emergency systems ... Sometimes ... one read 'engine starting' while being driven to dispersal; 'take-off procedures and speeds' while the engine was warming up; and things like flaps and landing speeds while in the air.

Anne Welch, *Happy to Fly*

Aetheris Avidi

(Eager for the Air)

Sealed in our singular cockpits –
awaiting the off or circling to land,
the skies were teeming with Spitfires,
or so it felt sometimes, birds wheeling
far below, dust beneath our wings.

Some days we couldn't fly –
the weather was often dubious
so we sat about in the mess, smoking,
chatting, playing cards or backgammon
until the skies had cleared.

We thrived on it, despite the danger –
despite the tedium of hanging around
waiting to fly or those washout days,
when it seemed like the wartime
grey would never brighten.

*We were just glad to be flying – doing
our bit doing something we loved.*

Keeping Our Feet on the Ground

We were just girls, some barely finished,
others trekking halfway across the world

for the chance to fly with the ATA.
With youth, that innate fearlessness

yet we knew it could happen to any of us –
the nose dives, the one-off engine failures,

getting caught in the ropes, but such gloomy
thoughts were a danger in themselves.

Pressure enough from the press and public
without putting our feelings on the line.

We had the ground in sight, but with a terrible
temptation to fly above the clouds, break free.

Grey Skies

Endless tapping
of rain on windows
echoed her impatient
hands stubbing out
one glistening end,
lighting another.

A washout – grey skies
limpid clouds and wind
gathering energy at one
corner of the airfield;
she sensed the trouble
it would bring.

She flicked her wrist
brushed her trousers
dreamed of clear skies,
eyes glazed by raindrops
beating a cascade down
the window pane.

Endless planes lining
a silver runway, invading
dreams, stealing her sleep,
hands stubbing out one
dead end, reaching
for yet another.

The Forecast Looks Doubtful

We relied on maps, the compass and the watch –
but often the weather intervened, kept us

grounded; playing cards, writing letters
we may never post, stirring stewed tea

disconsolate, waiting for the wind to die
down, for the sun to make an appearance.

It was grim when all we craved was to be
airborne, all other matters scudding far below.

There was the sky and there was only the sky.
And mostly, we hoped, there was just *our* sky.

ATA Cockpit Check

If we had a head for letters we were fine.
Can I remember the code…?
Let's see now, before take-off –
H, Double T, well that was
Hydraulics, Throttle Tension & Trim
M, Double P – ah yes,
Mixture, Pitch & Petrol
F, G^4, F – Flaps, Gills, Generators,
Gauges, Gyro & Fuel boosters
And there were three more I think…
U, S, T – Unlock controls, Superchargers,
Tail wheel lock. Check everything twice
before every take-off, the rest we managed
to remember in the sky. All clear – *Contact!*

Simply Bliss

For Mary Wilkins Ellis & Veronica Volkersz

I've flown many types of plane,
learnt the controls, read the notes –
but the Spitfire! Well, I mean,
it was just so *fast and furious,*
so delightful to fly.

I couldn't wait to get that chit,
then the day arrived and I drew a Spit –
so light to fly, such a snug cockpit
and such good fun!

You could go up and play with the clouds

I just loved speed, couldn't help it –
was delighted when I got that buff
envelope from ATA; eight months later
I was flying Hurricanes. But the Spitfire,
well I'd second Mary – *what* a thrill!

It was the perfect lady's aeroplane!

Chit: delivery or collection papers with details of each plane.

One Coat for the Plane, Several for the Pilot

Rosemary Rees felt the cold and would often send
someone else in with her chit, bundled in the plane,
shivering and freezing despite her many layers.

The winter of '39 was endless, up to Lossiemouth
and Prestwich in Tiger Moths, lifted out stiff to the bone,
fingers numb and useless. Then freezing train journeys
home to fly again the next day, and the next.

Rosemary had made a coat for her own plane, wrapped
in its hangar, kept safe from bird mess on the fuselage.
They shivered on through that long winter, through

the gathering clouds and mutterings from the press.
The layers added an extra skin, while 'that fellow Rees'
in the Anson remained a mystery to the Air Controllers,
hidden beneath her coats, rugs and fur tippets.

Former ballet dancer Rosemary Rees MBE, one of the First Eight, was second-in-command to Margot Gore at Hamble.

Four Miles to the Inch

Vital knowledge for visual contact –
following railway lines (a pilot's best friend),
clumps of trees (*they don't move*), or finding
familiar spires to mark landing strips.

Check in with the Met, check your map
tucked into your boots for easy access.
Never mark barrage balloons, never write
anything of interest to enemy eyes.

Develop a *passion for maps,* a knowledge
of the country's many towns and hills
(in particular *hills*). Maps imprinted
on the mind, keeping the ground in sight.

Maps that float into dreams, disturb your sleep.

Hush

Those silent moments,

Before the rain,

Scanning the skies

Hoping for a gap

In the clouds, knowing

It's closing in.

Rare moments flying above,

Illicitly, gaily, not knowing

If you'll find that gap

But hoping, praying

You'll arrive long before

The storm breaks.

Sound and Fury

The throb of engines

The reek of hot oil

The speed of danger

The fall from grace

The sense of an ending

Coming too soon,

Crashing, falling

Splintering

Silence

Beware the Barrage Balloons

Every pilot's nightmare, especially the cables –
they had a habit of moving overnight.

Not allowed to mark them on maps, we had
to fly at just the right height, no hit or miss.

Bell-shaped bollards held them down, kept us
on a level, give or take an inch or two.

But those inches mattered, as we all knew,
best to stick to the Charlie lane, fly on through.

There were some lanes the pilots knew were free of balloons including 'C' for Charlie.

Keep on Flying

We had to be selective in our thoughts up there –
whoever was dead or missing, we had to let them go
for the time being, at least.
Button up, keep flying.

If we let our emotions take over, we were lost –
those planes were our responsibility; it was our duty
to reach our destination, arrive in one piece …

No time for daydreaming, no time for 'what ifs' –
if we didn't focus on our controls the ground would
simply come rushing towards us …

SISTERS IN SPITFIRES

A Gathering of Doves

Leylands Farm, April 2015

From my open window, their flight
patterns are distinct, a precise hovering

before dropping en masse to land plumb
on their nesting and resting eaves.

Their wings catch the sun every time,
glinting, slicing through the sky.

They've lived and bred here for years,
circling through seasons, coming home.

Theirs is the long line of a pitched roof,
the free-falling, eye-catching descent.

From my desk, Carroll Gibbons vies with
Vera Lynn to keep my pen in the mood

as the doves show off their Spitfire dance,
spinning, diving, gathering, flying free.

Celebrating at L'Ecu de France, July 1941

We pooled our petrol coupons, a little light-headed,
we'd go tonight while the triumph was ours.

We piled into cars, applying lipstick and checking
our hair, this night deserved nothing less.

Navigating grey London streets, past all the latest
billboard news, we arrived on the dot of seven.

We were shown to our table in the darkened interior,
took a moment to catch our breath, look around,

before scanning stiff menus and raising our glasses
to our first Hurricane flights – Spitfires were next!

Spitfire Dance

Halfway between runway and romance,
mind trained firmly on the here and now,
that patch of sky ahead.

In limbo waiting to take off, sometimes dying
to land, it was a feat of balance, keeping
a weather eye on social ops.

He'd asked his dark-haired friend to look out
for her, dance after dance, claiming her
when he came off duty.

She'd approached the floor with caution,
wondering if this particular flight signalled
the start of the rest of her life.

3pm Appointment at Austin Reed

The devil was in the detail, every little detail.
I scanned myself in the mirror, head to toe,
automatically straightened my blue jacket,
smoothed down my already smooth hair,
checked my wings were firmly in place.

I sensed so many people watching me
behind the polished mirror, watching
and waiting for me to fall, to crash land
or just give up and go home, raise a family.
I drew myself up to my full 5′2″ – no way!

We were made to measure at Austin Reed,
tailored to aviation perfection. It was truly
our made-it moment; we'd proved ourselves
in flying hours and cross-country sorties.
we were ready to conquer the skies!

Chits for Chocolate

We collected our chits each morning
from a polished wooden shelf – the thrill
of a new plane would often keep us going.

It was decided we needed a little more for safe
energy levels, so when we returned our chits
we got a 2oz bar of Cadbury's Dairy Milk.

(This was all thanks to Dr Buchanan Barbour,
who persuaded the Ministry that us girls needed
chocolate – has it not always been the case?)

One pilot, it may have been Jackie, used hers to
send love letters, she'd wrap them in a note
and drop them from her Spitfire –

the finder was to keep the chocolate in return
for delivering the letter. It was such small things
that kept us going sometimes, it really was.

I AM the Pilot

One Wellington bomber safely delivered,
the ground crew stood waiting for the pilot.

Mary Wilkins Ellis, petite but more than capable
of flying military aircraft at more than 300 knots,

had delivered it solo – in combat the RAF used
a crew of six, with navigator and engineer.

She climbed through the hatch with her parachute,
surprised by their incredulous looks and by

the one who climbed back in to double check.
I AM the pilot she said – here's your plane.

First Officer Mary Wilkins Ellis delivered 400 Spitfires for the ATA, flew 76 types of plane and 1,000 aircraft overall. She was Managing Director of Sandown Airport on the Isle of Wight from 1950-70, the UK's first female Air Commandant.

That Magnificent Woman

Once doubled as Lady Penelope, flying
a Tiger Moth under a motorway bridge,
landing in court on seven separate charges.

She also flew a Demoiselle replica, starring
in a film about Magnificent Men, with many
flying hours under her wartime belt.

Joan had been Britain's youngest pilot at
seventeen, logging 600 hours by twenty-two;
ferrying seventy-five bombers for the ATA.

She once delivered a Halifax to Hamble –
dumping her parachute outside the control
room, she went to hand in her chit.

The duty pilot moved his gum from cheek
to cheek and asked for the pilot to sign in.
I *am* the pilot said Joan, here's your plane.

Joan Hughes MBE flew for almost fifty years. She retired in 1985 with 11,800 hours in her log book and two films to her name.

The Barracuda Queen

I just applied and I didn't think for a minute I'd be accepted ...
Annette Hill

They called me the Barracuda Queen, up where I was stationed, I just loved them! They'd let me know when one was in and I'd jump at the chance to go up in them. Not that I'd miss the chance to fly a Spitfire either – none of us girls would!

The Spitfire was a life unto its own; it was just beautiful...

Annette looks back with a twinkle, her younger self shining through, her passion for planes upmost in her mind – she couldn't get enough of the Barracudas.

And learning how to land, once airborne?

Well, it comes to those who wait...

Sharing the Guard's Van

Molly looks over her shoulder
and sees her younger self sharing
sandwiches with one of the chaps
in the guard's van, at Exeter, arriving
at Paddington in the early hours.

Soldiers were spilling onto platforms
and the guard offered her some peace;
she was relieved to rest on her parachute,
pleased to share tea and sandwiches
with a tall, friendly stranger.

They may not recall the conversation,
or if it was wet or windy that day,
but it remains an encounter, a shared
afternoon amid the flights and flurry,
the scattergun impressions of war.

First Officer Molly Rose OBE grew up in a flying family (Marshalls of Cambridge) and worked as a ground engineer before joining the ATA. She delivered 486 planes and flew 36 different types from 1942-45.

One Fine Day

I'd been told my first Spit was waiting at the airfield.
It was a day we all looked forward to, amid the sorties,
the bombs, the long days and the darkest of nights.

So one fine day I went to collect it, watched as it taxied
towards me, sun gilding its wings, catching it just so.

Here I was, my first Spit and out stepped the pilot,
but would you believe – just a slip of a girl!

There I was, put firmly in my place, but glad she'd
ferried it my way, glad to slip into her seat, to climb
and dive like a bird set free, on that vivid virgin flight.

Sisters in Spitfires

The only sisters to fly with ATA, Joy and Yvonne
were posted to different pools under different names
but shared an enduring love of the Spitfire.

A plane that turned many into poets and dreamers,
they flew with *wings sewn on their backs,* felt snug in
the cockpit, handling their Spits with care.

Joy jumped at the chance to join the ATA,
glad to be at Hamble in 1944, glad to learn to fly
ab initio before she could drive a car.

Older sister Yvonne, posted to less-than-glamorous
Cosford, flew in thick Midlands fog, but at least they
were both airborne, making it through the war.

'The Gough Girls' grew up near Cirencester in Gloucestershire; they delivered 103 Spitfires between them and flew eighteen different types of plane.

Snaking Down from Lossiemouth

Heavy, serge   curtains of night   a cloudless sky
rising moon   the only disc   of sparse light
Squatting   on her parachute   creaking, tired
the jolt & clamour   endless strangers   breaking
endless journeys   She pulled   her blue scarf
tight as they rolled   into the night,   winding
through blackout   blur of boundaries   all station
names obscured   Her dreams   disturbed by
nameless faces   in dark corridors   She shivered
in fitful sleep   waking to the   eternal pitch
the jolt & clamour   Endless   North to South
a change of train   but for now   time spinning
into sticky tar   the need for a bath   a hot cup
of tea, blankets   & sleep before   the next flight.

Flings of Fancy

Mad flings – some you can control,
some you can't, flights of fancy, flings
with wings. Younger flings – girls about
town, dashing around in a plane between
parties, flings with undesirables. Older flings –

acquiring new wings, fashionably late in life,
flings on horseback in your seventies, going
on eighty. Time to give up? Not at all –
time to recall, with the smallest of sighs,
all those flings that made you who you are today.

LEAVING LEGACIES

I miss the beauty of that world above the earth…
It is not I that feels that thrill,
Though yet the memory lingers still …

Jackie Moggridge, *Spitfire Girl*

Brooklands Swing

They're *in the mood* – swirling
the dance floor, hands skimming
hips, scarlet lipstick glossing, all
eye-linered nylons & vintage chic.

They're hovering at the stalls,
clustering rails, rummaging
period pieces, yellowing maps
offering up roads still to travel.

From the clubhouse balcony
classic cars slip into easy mono,
as Diana wafts by, Lettice strides
the other way, ready for the sky.

Spring sunlight dances back into
Brooklands, crowds lap nostalgia,
the glitz & glamour of bygone days
cheering races, applauding flights.

Remembering Jackie

Jackie danced with the wind – she flew by the seat
of her skirt, raised on a cushion, head in the clouds.

She loved to watch the sun appear, craved peace
and solitude, the sheer delight of soaring free.

Jackie showed her daughters petals unfurling, dew
glistening on grass, rain-splash on yellow roses.

They billowed under duvets, learning how to fly.

She wrote poems by streetlight, *longing to be a pin-up,*
she embraced her family, lived for fun and flight.

Jackie relaxed into headstands at Hamble, or turned
her morning somersaults, dark eyes shining.

She pushed boundaries with a tilt of her chin, longed
to break the sound barrier, flew Spitfires to Burma.

Captain Jackie was proud of her post-war wings –
paving the way for women with a *blazing Spitfire trail.*

Honor Salmon's Pale Blue Shirt

Hung in Diana's wardrobe for nearly fifty years,
brushing against her sway of silk dresses –

poignant memories of a pilot who helped
a novice before floundering on high ground,
caught in the English weather, almost home.

The pale blue wool was soft to the touch, much
softer than ATA issue, and fitted Diana perfectly.
Her family had wanted her things to be shared.

She burst into tears the only time she tried it on,
alone in her digs. Honor's blue-grey eyes twinkled
back from the mirror – it was too much to bear.

She remembered with pride the young First Officer
who befriended her, taking it down now and again,
shaking out the clouds, before slipping it back

between shot-silk blues. Honor's presence lingering,
her kindly words drifting down the decades.

First Officer Mrs Honor Isabel Salmon (granddaughter of Sir Isaac Pitman, developer of shorthand) died on 19 April 1943 aged thirty. Diana Barnato Walker never forgot her.

An Unmarked Grave

With a sharp Eton crop and a crisp sense
of humour, Connie was fearless in the skies –
spanning Europe in her Sopwith Grasshopper,
her Westland Widgeon and her Comper Swift.

*She completed her first solo flight in 1925 –
upside down.*

Undaunted she became one of the first
British women to gain a licence, the first to fly
on Tyneside, the first to skim the Alps in her
de Havilland Tiger Moth.

Rising to Flight Captain in the ATA,
Connie flew Spitfires and Lancasters from Hamble.
She didn't set out to break any world records, but
was a demon at backgammon in the mess.

She was remembered as *funny, feisty
and fiercely independent,* living with rescue donkeys
on her Tynedale farm, yet ready with the whisky
and Woodbines when friends came to call.

Her moorland grave is simply marked
with the stone from her outdoor pool, the notice
in the local paper written in Connie's own hand.
No fuss, no limelight – an extraordinary life.

Constance Ruth Leathart, 1903–1993

Mosquito Tears

Dora Lang was giving a lift to Flight Engineer
Janice Harrington; it seemed an ordinary day,
one more flight in her work for the ATA.

She would have focused her mind sharply
on her landing, as always, and she knew
Lasham well, her plane even better.

She was considered to be a pilot with flair,
sure and steady and particularly happy
that day, a sunny day like any other.

Yet in that moment before the stone drops,
akin to a horse rearing at rustling paper
or lashing out in a sudden temper,

their Mosquito bucked upon landing,
reared up and burst into flames. Those left
behind tried to stop the darkness from

descending, as they watched the draped
coffins through flickers of late autumn sun,
as they tried to comprehend.

Dora Lang and Janice Harrington are buried alongside each other at All Saints Cemetery, Maidenhead where there are a number of ATA and Armed Services graves.

On Such a Day

Our hearts sank when we guessed
the worst, or dared to let ourselves imagine…

On such a day, we stayed on the ground,
not wishing to tempt fate.

On such a day we looked upwards,
almost at the same minute, the same hour.

We couldn't help ourselves, automatically
scanning for any signs of life.

On such a day we stretched aching
muscles, pinching our flesh raw while

waiting for news that never fully surfaced.
We knew in our hearts she was gone.

"Amy Johnson is not only a loss to aviation: those who knew her have lost the type of friend who cannot be replaced." Pauline Gower, *The Times, 1941.*

Moving Up the Blackboard

For Operations Officer Alison King

The call came; the one we all dreaded,
when her voice would change, her eyes
take on that strained, faraway look.

She'd carefully cover the mouthpiece,
nod over in my direction and I'd lower
my eyes, try to stop my stomach falling.

Another one down, details as yet unknown.
Other lives and histories would be forever
changed at their loss; that we knew.

But for now, we had to log the details,
find a way to move on through the war,
to keep doing our bit up in the skies.

Even before she'd replaced the receiver,
I'd wiped the blackboard, filled in any gaps.
It was good for morale; it had to be done.

Tell Me

Tell me it wasn't in vain – the sorties,
the fight for recognition, the press attention,
endless ferrying from factories to frontline.

Tell me it wasn't in vain – encouraging
women in what was always a man's world.
(Did that really change, after the war?)

Tell me that my work and all those women
who joined the ATA, moved up the ranks,
kept their spirits up ... tell me we made
a lasting contribution.

Tell me that our losses weren't in vain –
that they signified in the toll of those years,
the endless death and destruction.

We set out to assist, to help release men
to fight and I trust we did a good job.
We were always eager to take part –
always eager for the air.

Pauline Gower MBE made huge strides for women in aviation. She died after giving birth to twin boys, aged thirty-seven. Her son, Michael Fahie, pays tribute to a remarkable woman in his book, A Harvest of Memories.

A Rapid Dispersal

We knew it was almost over; a few of us
posed to lay up the flag at White Waltham,
November '45, many had already gone.

We smiled into the distance, still young
but perhaps wondering if the most exciting
part of our lives was behind us. We knew not.

Some of us were more than ready to hang up
our uniforms, take down our golden wings –
we knew we'd done our bit and more.

For others it was a wrench. We were simply
expected to pick up our lives, our jobs,
our kitchen sinks. But on that bitter-sweet

winter's day, as Audrey Sale-Barker lowered
the flag, we knew we'd given our best years
to the skies and mostly seen it through.

Yet some part of us would emerge from stray
corners of chilly airfields; remembering
those we'd lost along the way.

The ATA flag was lowered for the last time at White Waltham airfield, November 30th 1945.

Postscript – Go Fly, Young Woman!

Climb in a cockpit, push yourself past barriers,
fly on past that little voice that says 'what, *me*?'
Why not?

Pauline Gower, driving force and irrepressible poet,
thought that all women should take flying lessons –
quite simply *the best antidote to the manifold neuroses
which beset modern women.*

Put my name forward, Freydis Sharland told her
brother, the Spitfire was her favourite too, but she flew
long after the war, won her RAF wings. Founder of the
British Women Pilots' Association, set up ten years after
the ATA disbanded, she helped keep the flag aloft.

So go fly, young women!

Climb in a cockpit, push yourself past barriers,
fly beyond your limits – yes, *you*!

And why not?

Bibliography

'Atapologia' in The Aeroplane, The Most Influential Aviation Journal in the World, February 2, 1940

A Harvest of Memories, The Life of Pauline Gower M.B.E., Michael Fahie, GMS Enterprises, 1995

Amy Johnson, Queen of the Air, Midge Gillies, Pheonix, 2003

ATA Girl, Memoirs of a Wartime Ferry Pilot, Rosemary du Cros, Frederick Muller Ltd., 1983

Contact! Britain! An American woman ferry pilot's life during WWII, Nancy Miller Livingston Stratford, 2010

Happy to Fly, Ann Welch, John Murray, 1983

High-Flying Women, A World History of Female Pilots, Alain Pelletier, Haynes Publishing, 2012

Golden Wings, Alison King, White Lion Publishers, 1975 (first published by C. Arthur Pearson Ltd, 1956)

Lettice Curtis, Her Autobiography, hardback, 2004, second edition published by Red Kite, 2014

Piffling Poems for Pilots, Pauline Gower, first published by John Hamilton Ltd, 1934

Spitfire Girl, My Life in the Sky, Jackie Moggridge, Head of Zeus, 2014 (Woman Pilot, Michael Joseph Ltd, 1957)

Spitfire, The History of Britain's Most Famous World War II Fighter, Robert Jackson, Parragon, 2010

Spitfire Women of World War II, Giles Whittell, HarperPress, 2007

Spreading My Wings, Diana Barnato Walker,
Grub Street, 2003

The Female Few, Spitfire Heroines of the Air Transport Auxiliary, Jacky Hyams, The History Press, 2012

The Spitfire Pocket Manual, All Marks in Service, 1939-1945, Air Ministry, Conway, 2010

Further Resources:

Maidenhead Heritage Centre
http://www.maidenheadheritage.org.uk/
Home of extensive ATA archive and a Spitfire simulator.

Solent Aviatrix – https://solentaviatrix.wordpress.com/
A site dedicated to women pilots of the Solent.

Air Transport Auxiliary – details of all ATA pilots
http://www.airtransportaux.com/history.html

Notes:

In 'Model Pilot, Model Lawn', the funeral memory was from fellow pilot June Gummer, 1999, reported by Wing Commander Alan Watkins in an article online at:
http://www.haddenhamairfieldhistory.co.uk/index.htm

Elizabeth Lucas Harrison MBE was kind enough to share her memories of Monique Agazarian, whose first coach trip was to visit Elizabeth's SOE war memorial in Valençay in May 1991.

In 'Taking Tea with Thomas Hardy', the epigraph is taken from Hardy's poem, 'At Tea', from 'Satires of Circumstance', and the